–THE GREAT BOOK OF–

Library of Congress Cataloging in Publication Data

Roberts, David, 1929-
    The great book of ships.

    Originally published under title: The wonder book
of ships.
    Includes index.
    SUMMARY: Introduces ships over the centuries from
reed boats to hovercraft.
    1. Ships—History—Juvenile literature.   [1. Ships—
History]   I. Groom, Keith.   II. Cohen, Catherine.
III. Title.
VM150.R62   1981   387.2'09   81-189
ISBN 0-86592-064-8   AACR1

Pages 2 and 3: Yachts in the Kiel races in West Germany.

Opposite: A fully rigged clipper.

–THE GREAT BOOK OF–
SHIPS

RAY ROURKE PUBLISHING COMPANY, INC
WINDERMERE, FLORIDA 32786

Contents

Editorial

Author David Roberts

Designer Keith Groom

Editor Catherine Cohen

Published by Ray Rourke Publishing Company, Inc.
Windermere, Florida 32786.
Copyright © 1980 Grisewood & Dempsey Ltd.
Copyright © 1981 Ray Rourke Publishing Company, Inc.

Ships

The oceans cover seventy per cent of the world's surface, and for thousands of years people have felt the lure of travel beyond their own shores. Many of the earliest small sailing boats were dangerous craft. Fierce storms sometimes wrecked them, drowning everyone on board. But gradually ships became much bigger, and journeys grew longer. The power of wind in sails gave way to steam, steam to oil and finally to the most modern ships of all, powered by nuclear energy.

From reed boats to hovercraft, this book describes some of the biggest ships, some of the fastest and some of the strangest; simple shapes which have been afloat for centuries, and ships which were never able to take to the sea. The development of the ship is the story of one of the oldest and most successful forms of transport in the world.

Aluminaut, a deep-sea salvage submarine. It recovered an unexploded nuclear bomb from the seabed off Spain — the most expensive salvage operation ever.

The First Ships

Thor Heyerdahl, a Norwegian interested in the migrations of people across the great oceans, set out to prove that very early vessels could have made spectacular voyages. His *Kon Tiki* was a raft made from lightweight balsawood, the logs lashed together with ropes of reed. He sailed it from Peru to the Polynesian island Raroia in the Pacific, 6800 km (4225 miles) in 101 days. *Ra II*, shown here, was the second of his reed ships (the first one sank) which sailed across the Atlantic. It proved that ancient Egyptians could have introduced reed boats and pyramids to Central America.

Boats have existed for thousands of years. Our forebears have been spreading around the world for tens, if not hundreds, of thousands of years. They reached some of the most remote places sooner than we once thought. The islands of the Mediterranean, for instance, were mostly populated by 7000 years ago. Australia was reached 25,000 years ago after at least one sea crossing of 80 kilometers (50 miles).

Bones of deep-sea fish found among remains of shore settlements show that Stone Age people regularly sailed out of sight of land. A sudden storm or unexpected current could have carried the foolhardy farther than they meant to go. But some, at least, of the early voyages of discovery must have been planned. There must have been enough confidence in ships, or perhaps it was fear of an enemy that persuaded people to set out from a world they knew to cross the unknown seas.

▼ An ancient Egyptian ship of nearly 5000 years ago. It was built up from blocks of wood pegged together. A taut rope or truss ran from stem to stern over crutches to stop the hull breaking in half when it was lifted by a high wave. The ship was steered by the stern oars, and a trestle mast could be raised to carry a big square sail.

Ships

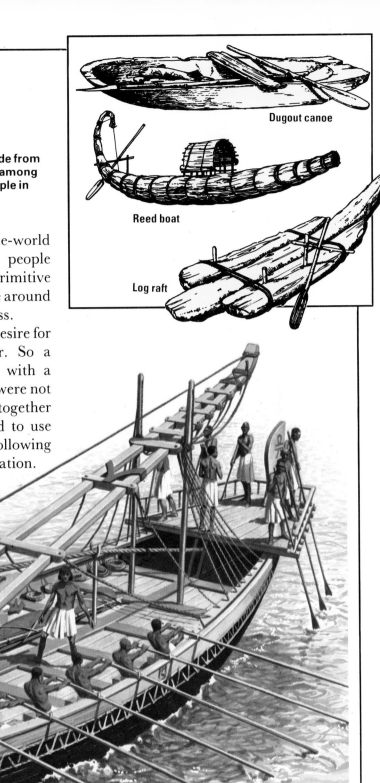

▶ A hollowed-out log or dugout, a boat made from bundles of reeds and a log raft. Such boats, among the first invented, are used by primitive people in remote places even today.

Dugout canoe

Reed boat

Log raft

In these days of round-the-world yachting, the daring of primitive people should not surprise us. Enough primitive boats and sailing ships are still in use around the world to prove their seaworthiness.

There has always been a human desire for things to grow bigger and better. So a dugout canoe became two canoes with a common deck, a catamaran. If logs were not to be had, bundles of reeds lashed together made good boats too. Man learned to use sails as a means of power, and following flights of birds began the art of navigation.

Into the Middle Ages

Ancient merchant ships were broad and high enough to carry as much cargo as possible and they could wait for a wind to drive them. Warships needed speed, whether there was a wind or not. They were long and lean with banks of oars to propel them as missiles against an enemy. This led to the invention of the keel, a solid wooden beam running the length of the ship and sticking out from the bow to make the head of the battering ram.

▼ In 1880, this Viking longship was dug out of the clay in Oslo Fiord, Norway, where it had lain for 1000 years. A full-sized copy was made and, in 1893, sailed across the Atlantic Ocean to America in a voyage of 28 days.

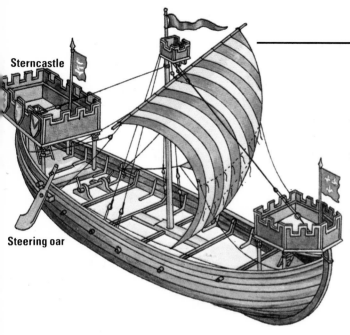

Sterncastle

Steering oar

(giving its name to the right-hand side of the ship) became too unwieldy as ships rose higher from the water. It was replaced by a rudder hinged to a sternpost and worked by a lever called the tiller. Even the tiller was soon put below deck and operated by a pulley system which led at last to the familiar ship's wheel.

Such were the ships, guided by the magnetic compass from China, which set out to explore the world.

The Viking longship was developed in the narrow fiords of Scandinavia, sheltered from the wind. There, it needed oarsmen. Out at sea, its single square sail could be set. The strong keel helped a longship to brave the worst storms; yet it could be rowed far up a river to launch a surprise attack on an inland town. The Norsemen raided throughout the Mediterranean in their longships and even discovered mainland America.

In ancient times, Mediterranean ships had adopted the Latin or lateen sail from the Arabs. It was triangular and mounted on a yardarm that could be swung to use a wind from almost any direction. Ships of the northern seas, the Baltic and Atlantic, stuck to the square sail until combinations of the two were tried and extra masts were added. A typical ship of the late Middle Ages might have a lateen sail on a mizzen or sternmast and square sails on the mainmast and foremast.

A lateen sail could help in the steering of a ship. The steering oar, called the steerboard or starboard

▲ A 14th century merchant cog fitted out for war with sterncastle and forecastle. Notice the square sail and the steerboard on the right.

▼ A 15th century carrack with foremast, mainmast and mizzenmast, able to carry square or lateen sails. Notice the hinged sternpost rudder.

Mainmast

Foremast

Mizzenmast

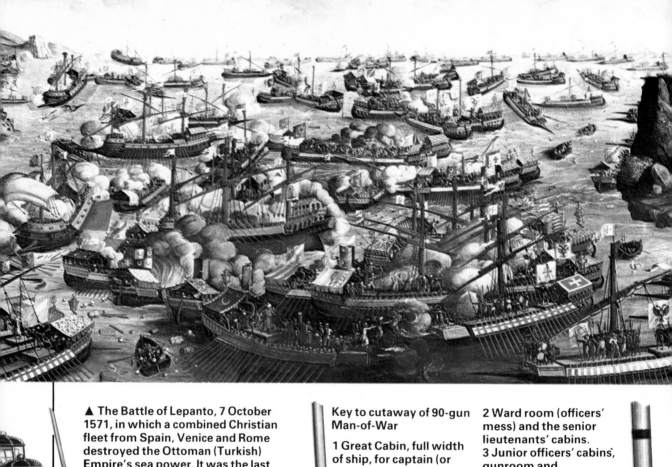

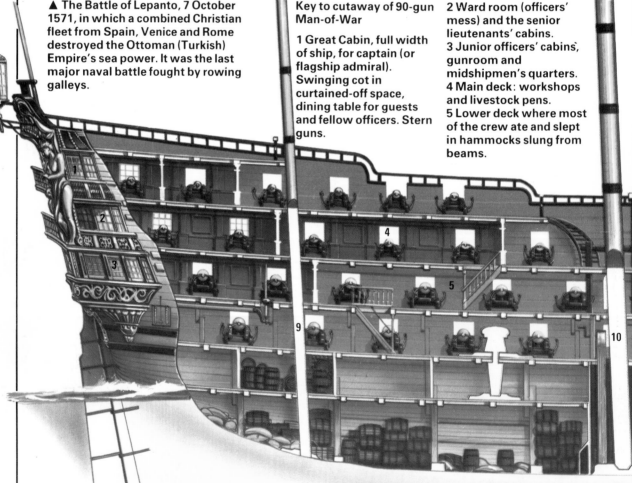

▲ The Battle of Lepanto, 7 October 1571, in which a combined Christian fleet from Spain, Venice and Rome destroyed the Ottoman (Turkish) Empire's sea power. It was the last major naval battle fought by rowing galleys.

Key to cutaway of 90-gun Man-of-War

1 Great Cabin, full width of ship, for captain (or flagship admiral). Swinging cot in curtained-off space, dining table for guests and fellow officers. Stern guns.

2 Ward room (officers' mess) and the senior lieutenants' cabins.
3 Junior officers' cabins, gunroom and midshipmen's quarters.
4 Main deck: workshops and livestock pens.
5 Lower deck where most of the crew ate and slept in hammocks slung from beams.

Battle for the Seas

In the 16th century men found guilty of crime were sometimes sentenced to be galley slaves. Ashore, they lived in barracks, well-fed and kept fit for work. They went to sea seldom and never for very long. Maneuvering or ramming an enemy in battle, they may have rowed hard for no more than ten minutes. They could be killed by the enemy or left chained to an oar in a sinking ship, but many survived long sentences.

The 18th century man-of-war, below, took men from jail or from merchant ships or used a press gang to kidnap them. On a long voyage, an average one-third died: of floggings, of scurvy caused by lack of vitamin C from fresh fruit and vegetables, of other diseases rife aboard.

All the skills of naval architecture went into the design of an 18th century ship-of-the-line. Of all its lavish decoration, painting and gilding at stem and stern, the figurehead was the most striking. Designed to identify the ship, it became its mascot, and like these here, was often kept after a ship had broken up.

6 Orlop deck where rest of crew messed and slept, very dark and with little air. In the stern was the cockpit where senior midshipmen slept. In action, it became the surgeon's casualty ward and operating theatre.
7 Storerooms, rope, and powder and shot lockers.
8 Main holds

9 Mizzenmast
10 Mainmast
11 Foremast
12 Forecastle
13 Ship's bell for signaling times of day and watches.
14 Galley with brick floor and chimney through forecastle deck.
15 Capstan for hauling on cordage and cables.

16 Beakhead with figure carved, painted and gilded, usually to represent the name of the ship.

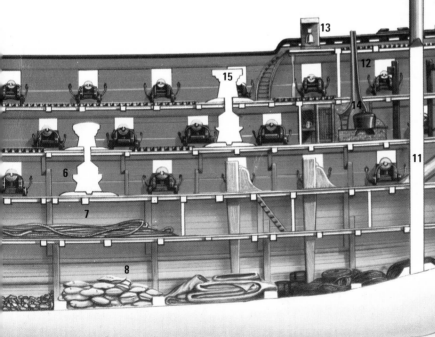

The Golden Age

The Great Clippers

The first true clipper, the US *Ann McKin*, built in Baltimore in 1832, was then the fastest thing afloat. British owners, anxious to keep the tea trade from China and India, followed the American example. The *Sir Lancelot* of 1865 could sail from Foochow, China, to the Lizard in Cornwall, England, in 85 days. But in 1869, America's first coast-to-coast railroad and the Suez Canal were both opened. One doomed round-the-Horn clipper trade. The other handed tea to the steamship. The clippers' brief glory was soon to be over.

The Parts of a Clipper Ship

The Spars This ship has three masts: **fore, main** and **mizzen**. Each mast is made of three parts: **lower, top** and, above, **topgallant** and **royal** all in one (sometimes two pieces). Between lower mast and topmast is a platform or **top**. Between topmast and topgallant is a **crosstree**. Slung across the masts are **yards** from which square sails hang. On lower mainmast and lower mizzenmast is a **gaff** at the top and a **boom** at the bottom, holding between them fore-and-aft sails. At the bow, a short **bowsprit** has a longer **jib-boom** above it.

The Sails On the jib-boom: 1 **fore topmast staysail**, 2 **jib**, 3 **flying jib**. On the foremast: 4 **foresail** or **fore course**, 5 **fore lower topsail**, 6 **fore upper topsail**, 7 **fore topgallant**, 8 **fore royal**.

Between fore and main: 9 **main topmast staysail**, 10 **main topgallant staysail**, 11 **main royal staysail**.

On the mainmast: 12 **mainsail** or **main course**, 13 **main lower topsail**, 14 **main upper topsail**, 15 **main topgallant**, 16 **main royal**.

Between main and mizzen: 17 **spencer**, 18 **mizzen topmast staysail**, 19 **mizzen topgallant staysail**.

On the mizzenmast: 20 **mizzensail** or **mizzen course**, 21 **mizzen lower topsail**, 22 **mizzen upper topsail**, 23 **mizzen topgallant**, 24 **mizzen royal**. Behind the mizzen: 25 **spanker**.

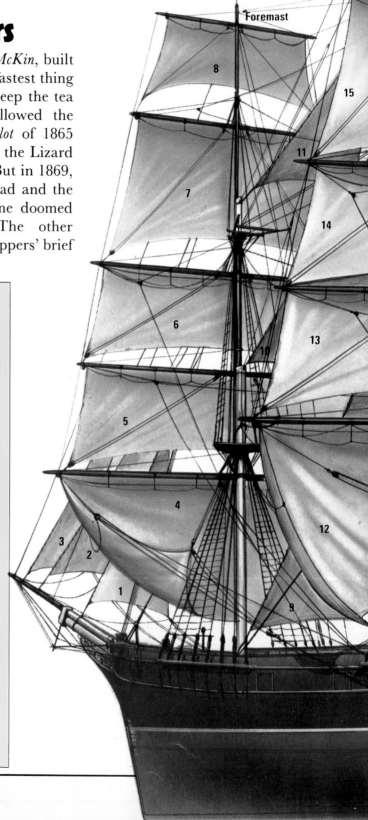

Mainmast

Mizzenmast

16

24

23

22

19

21

18

20

17

25

15

On the High Seas

From 1850, American and British ships were rivals for the tea trade to London and New York. The first of a season's cargo to arrive got the best prices, so the fast clippers came into being. They needed careful handling to get the best out of them. Captains were careful in the stowage of cargo and even trimmed ship by shifting iron cable from side to side. Large crews were needed to adjust sail to each new wind.

Flush-decked and designed to cut through a sea rather than ride it, clippers were always awash. To the cold and wet was added harsh treatment from the 'bucko' mates chosen for their ruthlessness in working the crew. As good seamen became reluctant to join a notorious ship, so the toughs and criminals replaced them, justifying ever more brutality. Many a fine spanking vessel was a hell-ship at heart.

Sailing ships must make up in fair winds for time lost in flat calms or when the wind is against them. Here are two of the most extreme solutions to the problem ever tried.

The fore-and-aft rig of schooners allow them to sail almost into the wind. On the principle of the more sails the better, the only seven-master schooner, the *Thomas W. Lawson* (top), was built. Though worked by a crew of only 15, she was never easy to handle and was wrecked in 1907.

The only five-masted square-sail ship ever built was the windjammer *Preussen*. Under full sail, as shown below, she presented well over an acre of canvas to the wind.

Clippers & Windjammers

Clipper ships were built for speed. A long slim hull, raked at the stem and with overhanging stern, presented the least possible area to the water. The American Baltimore clipper at first had two masts with fore-and-aft mainsails and square topsails. As clippers became fast carriers of such payloads as tea to London and New York and passengers to the gold rushes of California and Australia, they soon developed into bigger, three-masted vessels with square sails, ship-rigged as it was known. Yet, in the interests of speed, they were rarely heavier than 1000 tons.

Fast freight was lost to the railroads and steamships. Sailing ships had to be bigger to pay. Steel hulls were introduced for strength and easy maintenance. Speed was still needed to recover time lost in unfavorable winds. Masts grew taller to cram on every possible inch of canvas. Tonnage rose to 4000, even passed 5000 with the biggest sailing ship ever built, the *Preussen* (far left below). "Greyhound" clippers had become "workhorse" windjammers, like *Herzogin Cecilie* (right) which earned a living toting cargo until she was wrecked in 1936.

On 14 Feb 1895, the crew of the steamship *Ruapehu* were amazed to see sailing ship *Turakina* overhauling them. It proved that, even at such a late date, sail could beat steam, given the right weather conditions.

The Steam Era

▼ The *Charlotte Dundas*, built by William Symington in 1801, was a catamaran with boiler in one hull, engine in the other and a paddle-wheel between.

Early steamboats brought their inventors little joy. Boatmen were afraid for their jobs and smashed Denis Papin's 1707 boat. In 1783, the Marquis de Jouffroy's *Pyroscaphe* was successfully powered by the new Watt steam engine, but he won no backing for it. John Fitch ran his 1796 steam-paddled canoe for years on America's Delaware river, but killed himself when his backers abandoned him. The canal company that paid for *Charlotte Dundas* (left) let her rot and her inventor die in poverty.

Steam Power

Early steam engines worked by air pressure. Steam condensed to water in a cylinder, leaving a partial vacuum. The outside air pressure forced a piston into the cylinder. From the beginning, attempts were made to use the piston's movement to drive a boat. The first suitable engines were designed by James Watt, their separate condensers allowing the cylinder to remain hot while in operation. Watt himself thought high pressure steam was too dangerous. It was left to others to design high pressure engines small enough and with the power to carry a steamship first against river currents and then across the great oceans.

▶ The steamship *Great Western*, designed by Isambard Kingdom Brunel, reached New York four hours after *Sirius* (top far right), though she had left England four days later. Brunel followed that first success with the *Great Britain* and then, in 1858, the Great Eastern, shown here. The launch alone cost $280,000 which bankrupted the owners. Brunel died eight days after she began her maiden voyage, never knowing he had given her too little power, although she had sails, paddle-wheels and propellers.

▲ In 1926, sternwheeler *Delta Queen* was shipped in parts from Scotland to California. She used to work on the Sacramento river but now plies the Mississippi, a reminder of the old river queens.

▲ In 1838, *Sirius* became the first ship to steam all the way across the Atlantic. She managed the last few miles only by burning her spars to feed her furnace.

Robert Fulton was more successful with his *Clermont* which steamed 240 km (150 miles) from New York to Albany in 32 hours to win a Hudson river monopoly. He died in 1815 with 17 profitable steamboats on the Hudson and the Mississippi.

While America's rivers and lakes kept steamers busy, Britain took to the high seas. Steam packets were crossing the Irish Sea by 1818, the English Channel by 1819. And soon, oceangoing sailing ships carried auxiliary steam power.

Propellers

Early steamboats had paddle wheels. Ocean steamers carried sails as well. Most of a paddle wheel is out of the water, doing no work at all. In heavy seas, when a ship heeled over, one side wheel could be right out of the water, the other submerged and churning uselessly. A screw propeller, though much smaller than a paddle wheel, is wholly submerged with all its surface working against the water. Propellers were demonstrated in 1802 but were not widely accepted until the 1840s. In 1845, screw-propelled HMS *Rattler* won a tug-of-war against the equal-powered but paddle-driven HMS *Alecto*, proving the case to the British navy.

The Great Liners

Sirius and *Great Western* proved the value of steam, and two years later, Canadian Samuel Cunard opened the first transatlantic service. His paddle steamer *Britannia* left for New York from Liverpool on 4 July 1840 with 115 passengers and 230 tons of cargo.

From 1844, the Peninsular and Oriental Steam Navigation Company (P & O) ran a line from England via Gibraltar to Alexandria in Egypt, then by canal barge, Nile steamer and camelback to Suez and another steamship connection to India and China. The Royal Mail Steam Packet Company ran from England to Panama and, after an overland crossing, connected with the Pacific Steam Navigation Company for the US west coast or across the Pacific. In this way the great liners opened up the world to travelers.

Meanwhile, the Cunard Company had its first screw-propelled ship, *China*, in 1862, and its steam-turbined *Mauretania* won the Blue Riband Atlantic speed record in 1909 and held it for 21 years. Atlantic rivalry had begun.

The Unsinkable Titanic

She was the largest, most luxurious liner ever built, and thought to be the safest. Her hull, reinforced at the bottom and divided into 16 watertight compartments, could float with two of them flooded. On 14 April 1912, on her maiden voyage from Southampton to New York, at 11.45 pm, she struck an iceberg. Six hull compartments were ripped open. When her engines broke free and slid forward at 2.00 am, the *Titanic* nosedived. There were not enough lifeboats. 1513 passengers and crew drowned. Only 705 survived.

1 80-ton rudder
2 Starboard screw
3 Swimming pools
4 Cabins for crew
5 Revolving elevator for cars
6 Passenger cabins
7 Garage
8 Ballroom with balcony
9 Main lounge
10 Laundry
11 Engine room
12 Stabilizers
13 Boiler room

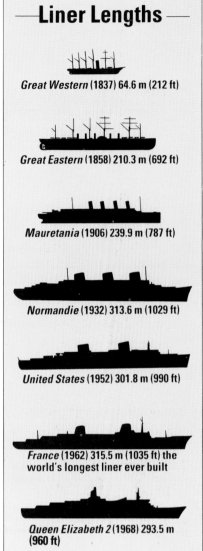

Liner Lengths

Great Western (1837) 64.6 m (212 ft)

Great Eastern (1858) 210.3 m (692 ft)

Mauretania (1906) 239.9 m (787 ft)

Normandie (1932) 313.6 m (1029 ft)

United States (1952) 301.8 m (990 ft)

France (1962) 315.5 m (1035 ft) the world's longest liner ever built

Queen Elizabeth 2 (1968) 293.5 m (960 ft)

▲ *Queen Elizabeth II*, launched in 1968 as a floating luxury hotel for 2025 passengers with a crew of 906 to look after them.

► As engine power increased, so did the size and luxury of the liners. Here some of the most famous are compared in outline.

Europa and *Bremen* won the Blue Riband for Germany, *Rex* for Italy and *Normandie* for France. Cunard won it back with *Queen Mary* in 1938, holding it for another 14 years. When America's *United States* crossed in 3 days 12 hours and 12 minutes in 1952, the last record, airlines were taking over.

The *Queen Elizabeth II* (below) was designed more for comfort than record-breaking speed. Her size may be gauged from the propeller (2), 18 feet across. She carries passengers' cars (5 & 7) and offers a ballroom (8), a theater (14), a ships's newspaper (17) and restaurants (18). Stabilizers (12) can reduce a 20° roll to 3°. Engines (11) use 525 tons of fuel a day at cruising speed of 28·5 knots. Thruster propellers in the bow (21) assist steering at low speeds. There is computer control from the bridge (20).

14 Theater
15 Main reception room
16 Hospital
17 Printing shop

18 Restaurant
19 Refrigerated storeroom
20 Bridge and chartroom
21 Bow thrusters
22 Bow anchor

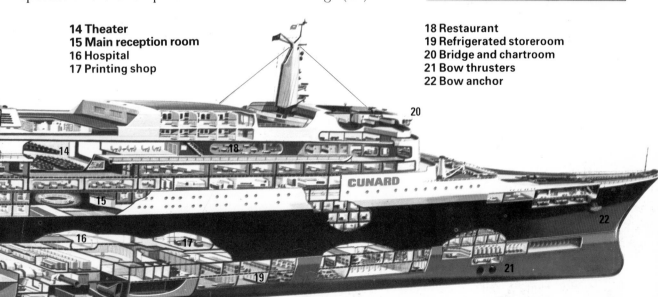

◄ Island people, living close to the sea, often express their awe of it in their art. This Japanese print shows an open boat lashed by huge waves, with land so near yet so far in that storm.

► Britain's J.M.W. Turner was another islander artist who depicted the sea in many moods. Here is a dramatic rescue from a small cutter caught on the rocks. His treatment of the wild movement of a rough sea is very different from that of the Japanese artist.

The fire that ravaged the freighter *Al Abbas* (below right) was put out and the wrecked ship towed into port. Even amid so much water, fire is one of the sea's most feared hazards. Cargoes are often highly inflammable, and fire can spread so fast that the crew can only abandon ship until the fire burns itself out.

Lost at Sea

- 4 December 1872: *Mary Celeste* found under sail with no one aboard: a mystery never solved.
- 24 July 1915: Great Lakes steamer *Eastland* in dock on Chicago river overturned, killing 812 day-trippers, including 22 whole families.
- 6 December 1917: French munitions ship *Mont Blanc* blew up after a collision in Halifax harbor, Canada. Worst-ever marine disaster: 1400 dead.
- 8 September 1934: Havana-New York pleasure cruiser *Morro Castle* caught fire killing 134 out of 548.
- 16 April 1947: ammonium nitrate cargo of French freighter *Grandcamp* exploded in dock at Texas City, Texas, setting off chemical and oil plants: 512 dead, over 3000 injured, $51 million damage.
- 22 September 1957: sail-trainer *Pamir* sunk in South Atlantic hurricane: 5 survivors from crew of 87.

Might of the Sea

Shipwreck!

When the volcanic island of Krakatao in Indonesia exploded in August 1883, it threw up a tidal wave 15 m (49 ft) high, which reached as far as Cape Horn, 12,510 km (7773 miles) away, before it subsided. Where it struck solid land, it overwhelmed whole villages, killing altogether over 35,000 people. Yet large ships, quite close to Krakatao at the time, were lifted by the wave and never even noticed its passing.

The sea is one of Nature's most powerful forces. Not even the rocks themselves can stand forever against it. But for many centuries, mankind has known how to build vessels that will ride out most of its furies.

The cockleshell ships of the great discoverers such as da Gama, Magellan and Columbus survived and so do the seemingly fragile round-the-world yachts of today. However, as the *Titanic* sadly demonstrated, no ship is unsinkable. Even where there are no icebergs, there is the danger of colliding with another ship in fog or darkness, running aground or breaking up against rocks.

Radio, radar and orbital weather satellites are among modern wonders that watch over our shipping. Ships are getting bigger and more numerous, and carry ever more dangerous cargoes. The oceans cover seven-tenths of the world's surface yet there are still crowded straits where a minor error can mean disaster.

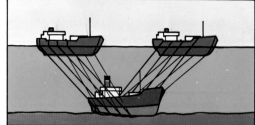

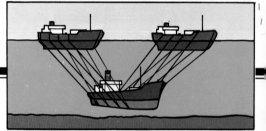

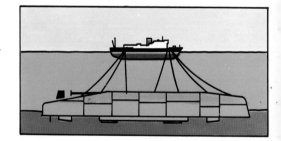

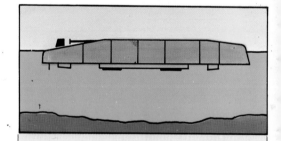

The underwater photograph above shows a diver guiding an old, encrusted anchor up to his surface vessel. He is using an aqualung, a cylinder of compressed air with breathing apparatus invented by French marine biologist Jacques Cousteau. Such light equipment has made exploring the strange world of the seabed easier and more popular. Archaeologists can dive to find out more than ever about ancient ships and cargoes, and they have found spectacular sunken treasures.

Salvage, of course, is often purely for profit. It could be worth raising a complete ship or the most valuable parts such as the engines. The cargo alone may be worth the expense of salvaging it. And it may be necessary to recover dangerous chemicals before they pollute the sea and kill the fish.

Diving bells and submarines can now work at greater depths than ever, using remote-controlled hands and closed circuit TV. Even so, finding a wreck can be a slow and frustrating business. The currents may move a sunken ship and cover it deep in sand, so that it may never be seen again. Nevertheless, diving and undersea work are often very exciting if always dangerous.

Raising a Wreck

A wreck in shallow water has cables run under it from one salvage vessel to another (top). At low tide, slack in the cables is taken up. As the tide rises, the salvage vessels and the wreck rise too (second picture). Buoyancy tanks, sunk filled with water and fixed to the wreck, can then be pumped full of air to raise it to the surface. If the whole hull can be sealed and filled with air (third picture), it will rise by it own buoyancy (bottom).

Treasure

▶ These gold items were aboard the *Gerona* when she sailed with the Spanish Armada to invade England in 1588. The English chased the defeated and fleeing Spanish galleons, into the North Sea and around the north of Scotland. In 1967, the Belgian archaeologist Robert Sténuit dived where local tradition claimed the *Gerona* had sunk. Here is just part of the amazing treasure which was at last brought to light.

▼ The *Torrey Canyon* was a big tanker which ran aground in rough weather off the southwest coast of England in 1967. Her cargo of oil spilled over miles of holiday beaches. Here, she is breaking up after she was towed into deeper water and bombed to sink her. Cargoes like oil are more economically carried in large quantities. This has led to bigger tankers which are difficult to maneuver in crowded waterways like the English Channel. The likelihood of a really horrendous disaster grows as the monster vessels carry their inflammable and poisonous cargoes along ever busier shipping lanes.

▲ The giant Japanese tanker *Igara* ran aground near Singapore. Salvage experts failed to float off the bows, so they used explosives to split the vessel in half. The rear section, with the engines, living accommodation and control equipment, is seen here being towed back to Japan. There, a new forward section was welded on to it, and the *Igara* is once again commissioned into the merchant marine.

Signs and

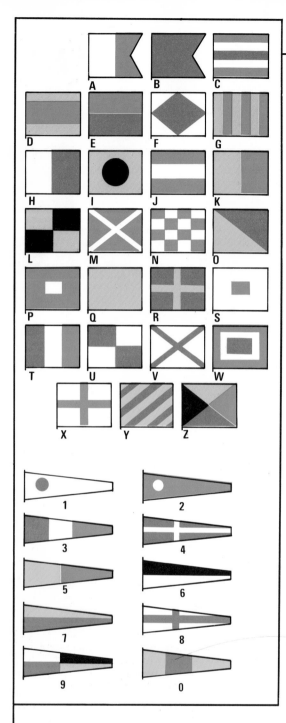

Traditional ways of signaling to and from ships at sea, that is without using modern radio or radar equipment, are with flags, lights or marker buoys. Each of the colored flags (left) stands for a letter of the alphabet, each pennant for a number from 0 to 9. One-, two-, three-, and four-letter signals can be made by using a code. The meanings of single letters are as follows:

A I have a diver below: keep clear
B Loading/discharging/carrying dangerous goods
C Yes
D I have steering difficulty: keep clear
E I am changing course to starboard
F I am disabled: communicate with me
G I need a pilot
H I have a pilot on board
I I am altering course to port
J I am on fire with dangerous cargo: keep clear
K I wish to communicate with you
L You should stop your vessel at once
M My vessel is stopped and making no way
N No
O Man overboard
P In harbor: about to put to sea
Q Quarantine
R I have lost speed: please pass
S My engines are full-speed astern
T I am trawling: keep clear
U You are running towards danger
V I need help
W I need medical help
X Stop what you intend: watch for my signal
Y I am dragging my anchor
Z I need a tug

▶ The position of the lights on a ship tell a watcher which way she is going. The side views on the near right show: top — a ship at **anchor; center – the red light shines on the left or port side;** bottom — a green light shines on the right or starboard side of a ship. In the diagrams on the far right, the lights **indicate: top — coming dead ahead; center —** crossing your port (left) bow; bottom — crossing your starboard (right) bow.

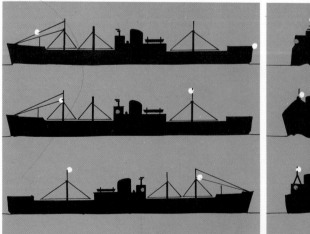

Signals

All ships must carry lights at night. A red light is always on the port or left-hand side of the ship and a green light on the starboard side. Thus a watcher far away can tell whether the ship is approaching or moving away. Ships also have lights on the mastheads arranged so that they are only visible from the front and a stern light that can only be seen from behind. The view of lights on a ship at anchor or passing by can be easily imagined from the diagrams below left.

Fires built on a cliff or a high rock have been a means of signaling to offshore ships for thousands of years. The Pharos lighthouse at Alexandria in Egypt was one of the Seven Wonders of the Ancient World. Today's lighthouses are often unmanned, automatic and remote-controlled. Each lighthouse has its own sequence of flashes, so that it can be easily identified.

There is a whole language of marker buoys, each shape and color having its own meaning to the seaman who has studied them. Buoys are in harbors and close outside, in shallow coastal waters and estuaries, and they are marked on charts. Many transmit a radio signal too, since they can not be seen in foggy weather.

Buoys

▶ Sometimes channels have two navigable arms. A red buoy with a black band means that the deeper channel lies to the right. A black buoy with a red band would mean that the deep channel was on the left.

▲ A green buoy marks a wreck: if it is conical you must pass on the left side, if can-shaped keep right of it. A yellow buoy marks a quarantine area.

▲ A red beacon with a white number marks the limits of the port channel; i.e. the channel would lie on the left of a ship coming into harbor. The right-hand limits of the channel are marked by black conical buoys with white letters.

▲ Beacons with horizontal red, white and black stripes mark shallow areas in the open sea. Black white and red beacons with a double cross on top mark the center of a channel or shipping lane.

◀ Lighthouses are the most ancient means of signaling from the shore to a ship. They may be on the mainland or on a rock or platform at sea. The tallest in the world today is this 106 m (348 ft) steel tower near Yokohama, Japan. Its light can be seen from 30 km (19 miles) away.

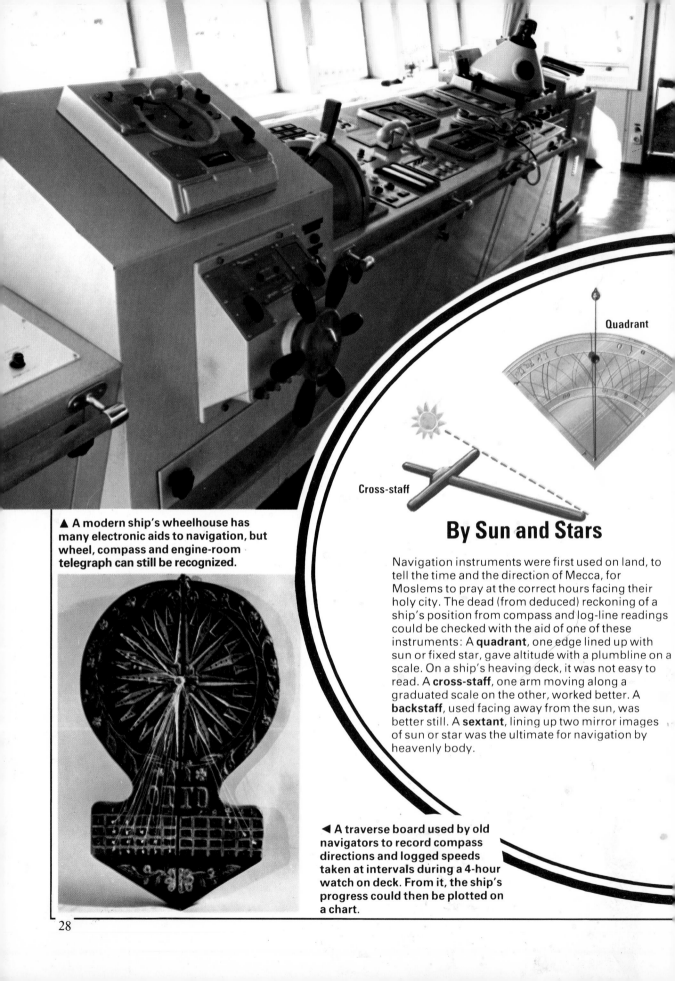

▲ A modern ship's wheelhouse has many electronic aids to navigation, but wheel, compass and engine-room telegraph can still be recognized.

Quadrant

Cross-staff

By Sun and Stars

Navigation instruments were first used on land, to tell the time and the direction of Mecca, for Moslems to pray at the correct hours facing their holy city. The dead (from deduced) reckoning of a ship's position from compass and log-line readings could be checked with the aid of one of these instruments: A **quadrant**, one edge lined up with sun or fixed star, gave altitude with a plumbline on a scale. On a ship's heaving deck, it was not easy to read. A **cross-staff**, one arm moving along a graduated scale on the other, worked better. A **backstaff**, used facing away from the sun, was better still. A **sextant**, lining up two mirror images of sun or star was the ultimate for navigation by heavenly body.

◀ A traverse board used by old navigators to record compass directions and logged speeds taken at intervals during a 4-hour watch on deck. From it, the ship's progress could then be plotted on a chart.

Navigation

The Age of Discovery really began with the great navigators, Christopher Columbus, Vasco da Gama, Ferdinand Magellan and many more. They navigated by the sun and the stars when the weather was clear. When it was not, they went by dead reckoning. A knotted rope thrown overboard was allowed to drag in the water and slip through the fingers. As they passed over the side, the number of knots was counted during a certain period timed by an hourglass. This gave the speed of the vessel. The magnetic compass, recently rediscovered, provided the direction. The two measures plotted a ship's progress.

Navigation by sun, stars and dead reckoning is still in use today. But now we can put a satellite into space so precisely that it will orbit at the same speed as the turning Earth. This means that it hovers over a particular point and can be used to check a ship's position. A series of such satellites transmits radio beams that can guide the world's shipping on its courses.

When the modern navigator has set the electronic equipment to put his ship on course, he can switch over to an automatic pilot. This system detects the smallest deviations in course and speed, making the necessary adjustments immediately. Meanwhile a radar beam is forever probing ahead, ready to warn of obstacles or other shipping that might become a danger. A ship may even be fitted with sonar equipment which sends sound waves to the seabed to "read" the surface and check position from an electronic map. We have come a long way from the patient sailor counting the knots as they pass between his work-hardened fingers.

Sextant

▶ Portuguese navigator Ferdinand Magellan was sent in 1519 by Charles V of Spain to discover a western route to the East Indies. His were the first European ships to sail across the Pacific Ocean which was named by him.

Fishing Boats

Fishing is as old as any other kind of hunting. The earliest boats must have been engaged in it. As Stone Age people became bolder, they ventured farther offshore and dropped their hooks into ever deeper water. The first seaside settlements must have grown around safe harbors where the primitive fishing fleets could be moored. Indeed, archaeologists have found evidence to support this in the piles of shells and fishbones they have unearthed alongside human habitations.

In some ways, fishing has remained comparatively simple when set beside the industrialization of other human activities. Most of the world's fishing fleets have merely replaced sail with diesel engines. The fairly recent introduction of the factory ship has vastly stepped up the pace of fishing, and the invention of the fish finger has increased demand.

▼ For fishermen who go to sea in small boats, life can be very hard. The partners in this trawler from Brittany for once have a rich haul to show for it.

Key to Trawler

1 Bow anchor and, on the deck above it, the winch for hauling it in.
2 Living accommodation for the crew. They may have to stay aboard in a remote fishing ground for weeks at a time. A freezer trawler does not return to its home port until its refrigerated hold is full.
3 Fishboxes are packed into crates kept in this refrigerated hold. Power for such a

Work

◄ The fishermen in this old Japanese woodcut spread nets from one boat to another. The are lowered and raised again to scoop a catch from near the surface. Fish is important in the diet of islanders like the Japanese.

▼ Freezer trawlers are beginning to drive out smaller fishing vessels. They freeze their own catches on board so the fish stays fresh all the way to the fish dealer. They stay longer at sea, bringing in bigger catches.

The world supply of fish lessens as the demand rises. Countries are extending the range of their territorial waters and putting limits on the size of catches. As the fishing fleets strive for more efficiency, their activities are being restricted. Their whole future is in doubt. There may soon come a time when each country will only fish its own waters, with fish-farms taking in enclosed stretches of shorelines.

Meanwhile, marine biologists lead the fleets farther from their traditional fishing grounds and into ever deeper water. Some of the fish brought up from these depths look very strange indeed.

large deep-freeze is provided by the main engine.

4 A trawler cannot keep to regular routes while it follows the shoals of fish. It carries radar to warn it of the approach of other ships in bad visibility. It may also have sonar equipment sending sound waves in search of the migrating shoals of fish.

5 A powerful winch hauls the loaded trawl over the stern ramp.

6 Next to the refrigerated hold, fishboxes are packed into crates.

7 Fish from the trawl starts its conveyor belt journey. It may be cleaned, filleted, salted, and finally packed.

8 A diesel engine drives the ship and powers the refrigeration plant.

9 High gantries are the cranes that haul catches aboard and move them about the deck.

10 The stern ramp, down which the trawling nets are lowered into the sea. The loaded trawls are winched inboard across it.

The Colossal Carriers

In recent years, ships have grown bigger while the crews to man them have grown smaller in number. The biggest of all, the supertankers, are not only the biggest ships, but the biggest vehicles of any kind. Yet less than forty men are needed to work them. They are ungainly things, requiring radar and computers to work out their movements far ahead and to adjust course and speed in time. They are too large for most docks. They are loaded and off-loaded by pipeline while anchored offshore.

While mail and light cargo have been taken over by airlines, ships have become bigger to take more cargo because it becomes cheaper per ton to carry. Many new ships have been built for special cargoes. There are refrigerated ships to carry perishable foodstuffs and gases frozen into liquids. There are container ships that link with road and rail depots for onward transport by land, even barge-carriers linking with the inland waterways.

On the right, two modern monsters are compared with a naval destroyer and a trimaran, one of the earliest seagoing vessels ever devised.

Container Ship
Length: 291 m (946 ft); width: 28 m (92 ft); speed: 28 knots; crew: 30

Hunter Killer Destroyer
Length: 161 m (529 ft); width: 17 m (55 ft); speed: 32 knots; crew: 296

◀ The transportation of goods packed in containers carried by sea, rail or road has rightly been heralded as a revolution. Individual containers need not be opened before their final destination. Meanwhile, handling is greatly simplified by their standard size. Here, a container ship is tied up alongside the moving gantry, with its battery of cranes which unload some containers while loading others at the same time. A new development is LASH (Lighter Aboard Ship) where containers are floating barges or lighters which can carry goods from a sea-going ship along the inland waterways.

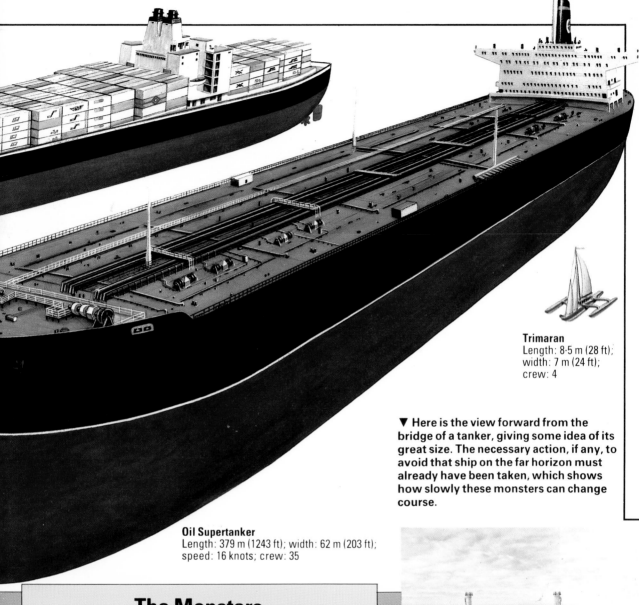

Trimaran
Length: 8·5 m (28 ft);
width: 7 m (24 ft);
crew: 4

▼ Here is the view forward from the bridge of a tanker, giving some idea of its great size. The necessary action, if any, to avoid that ship on the far horizon must already have been taken, which shows how slowly these monsters can change course.

Oil Supertanker
Length: 379 m (1243 ft); width: 62 m (203 ft);
speed: 16 knots; crew: 35

The Monsters

- The world's largest submarine is the nuclear-powered USS *Ohio*: 18,700 tons, 170 m (560 ft) long.
- The world's largest passenger liner is *Queen Elizabeth II*: 67,060 tons, 293 m (1000 ft) long.
- The world's largest aircraft carrier is the USS *Nimitz*: 92,800 tons, 332 m (1088 ft) long. The USS *Enterprise* is longer but of less tonnage.
- The world's largest battleship is the USS *New Jersey*: 59,900 tons, 270 m (885 ft) long.
- The world's largest dry cargo ship is the Swedish *Svealand*: 287,000 tons, 338 m (1100 ft) long.
- The world's largest ship of any kind is the French tanker *Pierre Guillaumat*: 563,908 tons, 414 m (1359 ft) long, which was completed in 1977. Globtik Tankers of the USA have ordered two 600,000-ton tankers for delivery in 1985.

Warships

The first all-iron warship was Britain's HMS *Warrior* of 1861. That year, the southern US Confederates bolted iron plates on to the wooden ship *Merrimack* and renamed her *Virginia*. In 1862, the Northern Union launched *Monitor*, an all iron ship with the world's first revolving gun turret. The two enemy ironclads met at Hampton Roads, Virginia, to bounce a few shells off each other, without doing any damage.

But it was a beginning. In World War 1, whole fleets of armor-plated warships fired at each other massive shells from huge guns over what were then incredible distances. World War 2 probably saw the last of the great pitched battles. Modern warships, too vulnerable to guided missiles, now have only a local role to play.

Superstructure.
The bridge, navigation room, flight control, radar, radio transmitters and receivers must take up as little deck space as possible.

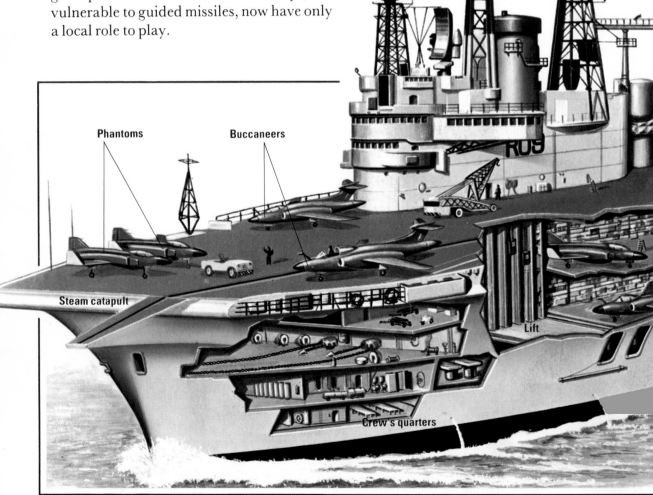

Phantoms

Buccaneers

Steam catapult

Lift

Crew's quarters

► This modern naval destroyer is a complicated package of electronics, with computer-controlled guided missile system, radar and sonar detecting devices and a helicopter for scouting missions. She has steam turbine engines to give her cruising speed; gas turbine for top speed.

◄ An early battleship, Britain's HMS *Dreadnought* (launched 1906), carried ten 12-inch and twenty-four 3-inch guns and five torpedo tubes. Her biggest guns fired 3000 lb shells over a range of 8 miles, though with no target guidance system.

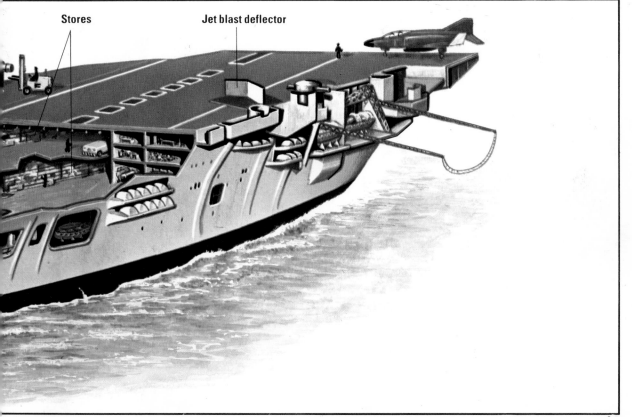

Stores

Jet blast deflector

Submarines

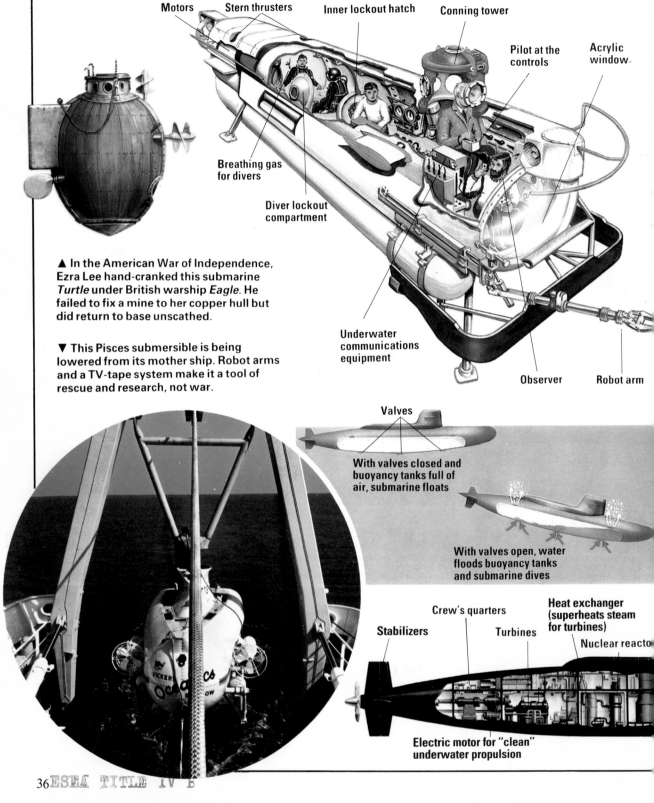

A Diver Lockout Submersible

- Motors
- Stern thrusters
- Inner lockout hatch
- Conning tower
- Pilot at the controls
- Acrylic window
- Breathing gas for divers
- Diver lockout compartment
- Underwater communications equipment
- Observer
- Robot arm

▲ In the American War of Independence, Ezra Lee hand-cranked this submarine *Turtle* under British warship *Eagle*. He failed to fix a mine to her copper hull but did return to base unscathed.

▼ This Pisces submersible is being lowered from its mother ship. Robot arms and a TV-tape system make it a tool of rescue and research, not war.

Valves

With valves closed and buoyancy tanks full of air, submarine floats

With valves open, water floods buoyancy tanks and submarine dives

- Stabilizers
- Crew's quarters
- Turbines
- Heat exchanger (superheats steam for turbines)
- Nuclear reacto
- Electric motor for "clean" underwater propulsion

In 1624, Dutchman Cornelius Drebbel demonstrated an underwater boat rowed by twelve oarsmen. In 1775, American David Bushnell launched *Turtle* (far left) which was operated by hand-cranked screws. Then in 1801, Robert Fulton (page 19) remained submerged for four hours in his *Nautilus*, propelling it with jets of compressed air. None of these was a true submarine. Limited to short periods underwater, they were merely submersibles.

Irishman John Philip Holland built a true submarine in 1898. Its gasoline engine was used on the surface and charged batteries for an electric motor which was used under the water. In World War 2, Germany produced the snorkel, breathing tubes poking up above the surface from a submarine just below it. Finally, nuclear power, needing no oxygen and creating no fumes, at last allowed submarines to stay under water for months at a time.

Submersibles are still in use by divers. The lockout submersible (left) has two compartments: one for the pilot is kept at surface air pressure, the other for the divers is adjusted to the sea pressure at the level they will leave the craft to work outside it.

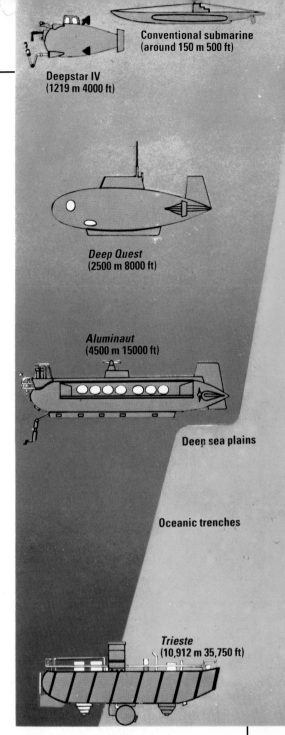

Conventional submarine
(around 150 m 500 ft)

Deepstar IV
(1219 m 4000 ft)

Deep Quest
(2500 m 8000 ft)

Aluminaut
(4500 m 15000 ft)

Deep sea plains

Oceanic trenches

Trieste
(10,912 m 35,750 ft)

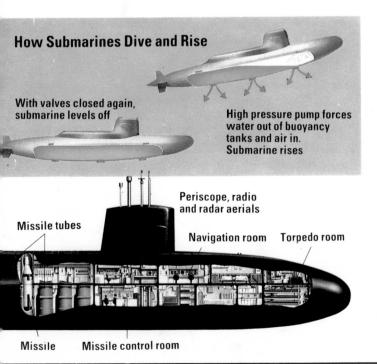

How Submarines Dive and Rise

With valves closed again, submarine levels off

High pressure pump forces water out of buoyancy tanks and air in. Submarine rises

Missile tubes

Periscope, radio and radar aerials

Navigation room   Torpedo room

Missile   Missile control room

▲ Submarines are designed to work at particular depths. *Trieste* has reached the deepest level of the ocean bed, Challenger Deep. The crew sit in the small spherical observation cabin under a large hull with its buoyancy (rising) and ballast (diving) tanks.

◄ A modern missile-firing, nuclear-powered submarine.

Strange Ships

Specialist Ships

The great liners and supertankers may seem very grand, but they need the work of lesser vessels to keep their sea-lanes open. Every port has its busy tugboats. They look small, but they have powerful engines to push and pull the big ships to and from their moorings. Dredgers seem to stand still, crawling at a snail's pace as they suck up or cut out the channels for those of deeper draught. Some places need icebreakers to keep the ports open throughout the winter. When their mighty engines cannot ram a way by main force, then explosives are used. There are even ships whose task it is to find icebergs and to tow them out of the way of other shipping.

Mankind is always adding to its knowledge of the sea. Most nations provide funds for research and to build special ships to undertake it. Ships also have their part to play in maintaining communications by laying the cables which wire up the world.

◄ On the move, this Flip Research Platform behaves like a normal vessel. When it reaches the area to be investigated, the bows flip up on end, and the stern becomes an underwater research station.

▼ This giant dredger is designed to clear muddy silt from a channel or dock area. As it moves ahead at a steady two knots, powerful scoops cut a 30-metre (100-ft) wide trench. The mud is carried far out to one side by the long boom.

▶ On the rim of the Arctic icecap, mountains of ice often break away to drift south on the prevailing currents. It could take months for them to melt. Meanwhile, they become a hazard in foggy weather along the shipping lanes. Here, a vast island of ice is being towed out of the danger zone.

▼ This is the USSR's *Lenin*, the world's first nuclear ice-breaker. Her reactor uses very little fuel, so voyages a year long are possible before refueling. She can cut through ice two meters thick. In January 1973, she took an expedition from Siberia to Murmansk in northwest Russia, an "impossible" winter trip.

▶ One of the vast cable tanks on board *Mercury*, a ship specializing in the laying of undersea communications cables. This one tank can hold nearly 3000 km (1850 miles) of cable.

The hull of this weird vessel of 1896 was lifted out of the water by hollow wheels revolving on either side. It was driven along by a screw propeller. The idea was that the turning wheels would slide easily through the water, but it did not work.

◄ English inventor and tycoon Henry Bessemer designed his own good ship *Bessemer*. The hull could roll in a high sea while the passengers were kept on an even keel by hydraulic machinery. It did not prevent pitching, it frightened the public and the crew found it difficult to handle.

Bizarre Ships

Most of the strange designs for ships have involved attempts to reach the perfect shape for the hull. One aim has been to find a shape that was stable whatever the winds or waves could do to it. Another was to lessen the drag or clinging effect of water against the hull reducing the vessel's speed. Successful hull-shapes have been arrived at in two ways: by the trial and error method used by primitive people over thousands of years, and by the scientific testing of models in tanks. Both methods have produced some beautiful, complicated, and bizarre lines.

▲ The *Connector* was really three sailing ships hinged together with steam power in the rear one. Versions are still being tried today.

▶ This craft, built around a souvenir of Ancient Egypt, a stone monument 20 metres (65 ft) high, was towed back to England. It nearly sank, was lost and found again, and the monument was finally erected by London's Thames river and is known as Cleopatra's Needle. The vessel, having done its job, was left to rust away in the Thames mud.

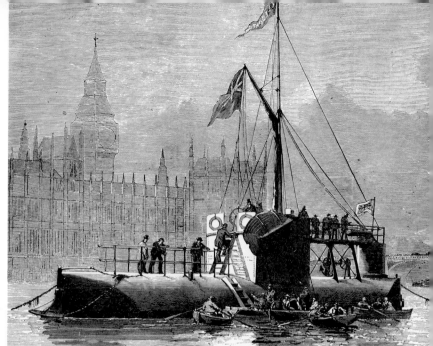

▼ The Russian *Novgorod* of 1873 was a circular ironclad designed for coastal defence in shallow waters. Steered by six propellers round the circumference, it was hard to keep steady while firing the guns. The American cigar ship (bottom), launched in 1866, had a similar lack of basic stability.

CONNECTOR

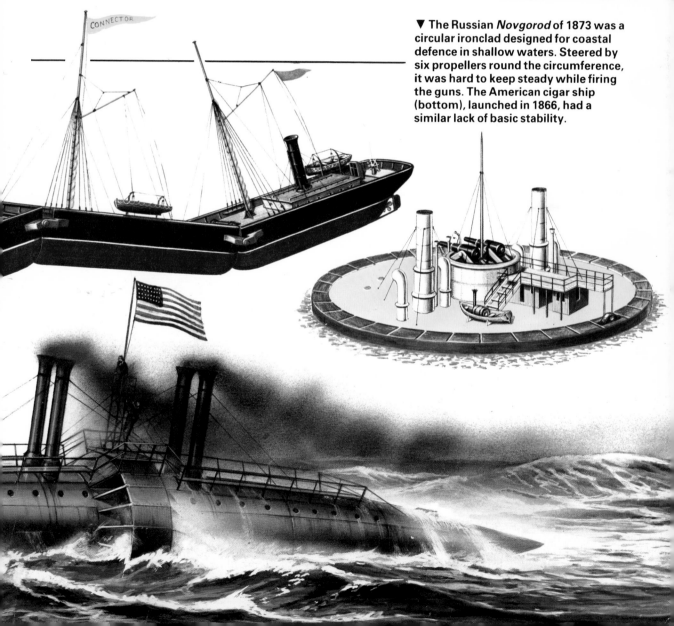

Racing on Air

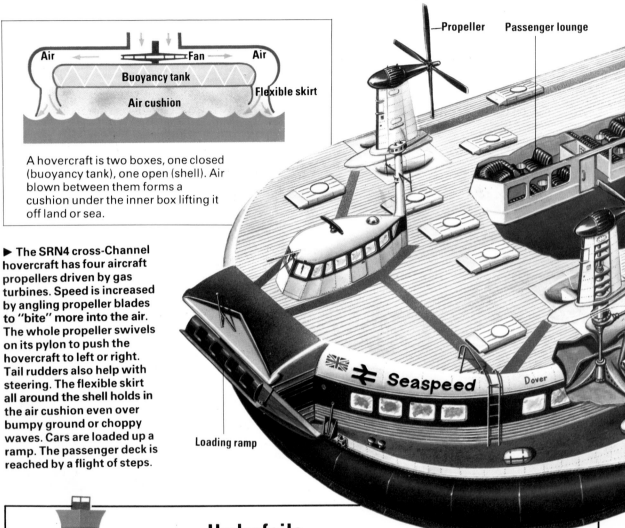

A hovercraft is two boxes, one closed (buoyancy tank), one open (shell). Air blown between them forms a cushion under the inner box lifting it off land or sea.

Air ← | → **Fan** | **Air** →
Buoyancy tank
Air cushion
Flexible skirt

▶ The SRN4 cross-Channel hovercraft has four aircraft propellers driven by gas turbines. Speed is increased by angling propeller blades to "bite" more into the air. The whole propeller swivels on its pylon to push the hovercraft to left or right. Tail rudders also help with steering. The flexible skirt all around the shell holds in the air cushion even over bumpy ground or choppy waves. Cars are loaded up a ramp. The passenger deck is reached by a flight of steps.

Propeller   Passenger lounge

Seaspeed   Dover

Loading ramp

Hydrofoils

There are two basic kinds of hydrofoils. In one, the foil breaks the surface of the water (top left). This makes it act as a stabilizer in smooth water as, for example, on a lake. In a rough sea, it has an opposite effect, making the craft even more unstable. The second kind of foil is totally submerged (below). It works only when it includes an adjustable aileron, like the hinged aileron in an airplane wing. This kind of hydrofoil craft carries a computer which makes continual fine adjustments to the aileron angle.

▲ A passenger hydrofoil speeding between the China Sea islands of Hong Kong and Macao.

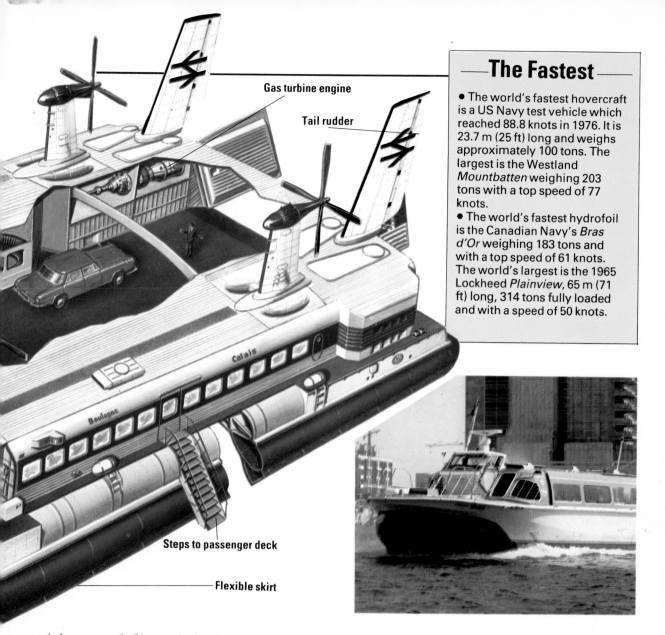

Gas turbine engine

Tail rudder

Calais

Boulogne

Steps to passenger deck

Flexible skirt

A hovercraft flies only in the sense that it is lifted off the ground or water by a cushion of air blown under it by a fan and held in by a skirt. Hovercraft can be driven along by aircraft-type propellers, and can move freely to and fro between land and water. Another kind has a flexible skirt only at bow and stern. The sidewalls are rigid like keels and dip into the water. These keels have screw propellers like a ship's. This kind of hovercraft cannot leave the water, but is quieter than the aircraft-propeller type.

A hydrofoil craft also works only in water. Unlike a hovercraft, it is never lifted up while it is stationary. Like an aeroplane, it

A hovercraft with rigid sidewalls. These slice through the water like the keels of ships. They are fitted with screw propellers or with water jet propulsion and are very quiet.

needs to gather speed in order to take off. In the stationary position, it is just a boat with the hull of a boat resting in the water. Its foils act like the wings of an airplane. As a wing gives lift when moving fast through the air, so a hydrofoil gives lift when moving fast through water. When a hydrofoil craft slackens speed, it settles back again into the water, becoming an ordinary boat once more.

Traditional Boats

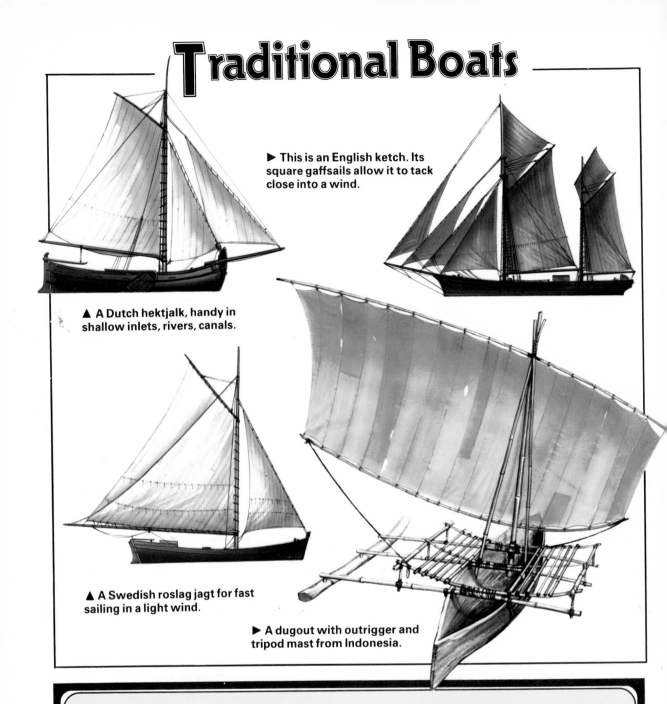

▶ This is an English ketch. Its square gaffsails allow it to tack close into a wind.

▲ A Dutch hektjalk, handy in shallow inlets, rivers, canals.

▲ A Swedish roslag jagt for fast sailing in a light wind.

▶ A dugout with outrigger and tripod mast from Indonesia.

Shipping, unlike other forms of transport, rarely discards its past successes. There are in the world today ships and boats to represent every kind ever known. The marsh Arabs still use reed boats. Rafts and dugouts are common around the Pacific. Eskimoes still use kayaks, North American Indians canoes. Sternwheelers still ply the rivers of North America. There are windjammers as sailing schools and schooners in the cargo trade.

The more we mind the boredom and irritations of supertravel, the more we go back to the old ways. We ride horses. We ski, skate and cycle. Increasingly we paddle in a pond, row on a river or sail in the sea.

Index

Acknowledgements

Photographs: Cover National Maritime Museum *top left*, British Hovercraft Corporation *top right*, P & O Lines *below right*; Endpapers ZEFA; 8 George Allen & Unwin Ltd.: *The Ra Expedition* by Thor Heyerdahl; 12, 13 and 16 National Maritime Museum; 16-17 P & O Lines; 19 USTS; 20 BBC Hulton Picture Library; 21 Cunard; 22 Victoria and Albert Museum *left*, Tate Gallery *center*; 22-23 Science Museum; 25 Ulster Museum, Belfast *top*, The Salvage Association; 27 Maritime Safety Agency, Tokyo; 28 Sperry Marine Systems *top*, Walter Luden *below*; 29 C.O.I.; 30 ZEFA *left*, Victoria and Albert Museum *right*; 32 Vickers; 33 Sperry Marine Systems; 35 Science Museum *left*, Keystone *right*; 36 Vickers; 38 Scripps Institute, California; 39 Marex *top right*, Novosti *center left*, Cable & Wireless *center right*; 40 and 41 Mary Evans Picture Library; 42 C.O.I.; 43 Hovermarine Transport Ltd.
Picture research: Penny Warn and Jackie Cookson.
Artwork: Tom Brittain, Mike Saunders, Brian Pearce, Michael Trim, Bernard Robinson, Ross Wardle, Norman Cumming, Michael O'Rourke, Douglas Harker.